WHISPERED PRAYER
MAMA SUSAN AND THE ORPHANS OF SUDAN

WRITTEN BY
LYLA PETERSON

Front cover photograph by Nate Grubbs
Back cover photograph by Toby Brooks
Cover and interior design by Casey Schilperoort

Dedicated to Susan Tabia.

Thank you for your faith.
It is more precious than gold that perishes.
(I Peter 1:6-7)

CONTENTS

INTRODUCTION

I took my first trip to Africa after retiring from my nursing career. In December 2006, I joined a team led by Dan Holcomb of Lahash International, a missions organization based in Portland, Oregon. The other team members were all much younger than I, yet I was eager to go. I appreciated Dan's first-hand knowledge of Africa, gained during his years growing up there. I was also drawn to the low-cost grassroots nature of the trip, and looked forward to visiting four different countries.

It was on this first trip that I met Mama Susan Tabia. Her profound influence on my life sparked a passion in me to learn much more about her story, about the culture and struggles of people in Uganda and Sudan, and about ways to maintain a connection between my life and theirs.

Before that first trip, I had learned about the years of unrest and upheaval in Sudan and northern Uganda: the Sudanese civil war and its "Lost Boys," the genocide in Darfur, and the terrorizing of children by the Lord's Resistance Army (LRA). I participated in some events to raise awareness of this country in crisis, yet was unprepared for what I would experience in my travels there. The time I spent with Mama Susan and those in her care opened my heart to the Sudanese people in a deeply personal way.

At the time of this writing, I have made a total of three trips to East Africa, connecting with Mama Susan and her projects each time. Mama Susan's life is marked by losses, fears, and struggles that few of us could imagine enduring. She has chosen to spend her life surrounded by widows and orphans in desperate need. Yet in the face of countless challenges, her life is characterized by the peace of Christ. As a beautiful reflection of her Savior, she freely pours into the lives of others from an abundance of faith, hope, and love.

In one of her emails to me, Mama Susan shared a favorite scripture from the book of Nehemiah. About Nehemiah 2:17-18, she says, "When Nehemiah shared his vision with others they replied, 'Let us start rebuilding,' so they began this good work." Jerusalem lay in ruins with its gates burned and its walls torn down. This description fits the country of Sudan both physically and spiritually. Like Nehemiah, Susan is hopeful that many people will join in the effort to rebuild lives and communities ravaged by war.

Although my connection to Mama Susan began when I met her in person, I pray that many more will connect with her life story, vision, and ministry through this book. I share my own experiences as a testimony to the ways God has changed me through her influence. I trust that there are many more connections to be made between Americans and East Africans through Mama Susan Tabia and her work in Uganda and Sudan.

KAJO KEJI, SUDAN

SUDAN

ADJUMANI, UGANDA

KAMPALA, UGANDA

UGANDA

KENYA

1

DREAMING DREAMS
Beginnings in Adjumani

"...I will pour out My Spirit on all flesh; Your sons and your daughters shall prophesy, Your old men shall dream dreams, Your young men shall see visions. And also on My menservants and on My maidservants I will pour out My Spirit in those days." – Joel 2:28-29

She arrived in Northern Uganda with few personal belongings, a middle-aged Sudanese widow in poor health. She had never been there before and had no family in the area. She had no place to stay. But she came looking for the children she knew were suffering there: Sudanese war orphans with no one to care for them.

Susan Tabia had been living in Kenya. On four separate occasions, she dreamed that there were children suffering in the refugee camps in Adjumani, Northern Uganda, and that she was to go find and help them. She resisted the dreams, and flew instead to Cairo, Egypt, to visit her younger sister, Naomi. After hearing about Susan's dreams – and her resistance to them – Naomi believed that God was indeed calling Susan to travel to Adjumani. She tried to convince her to go look for the orphaned children, even offering to pay her airfare.

Susan's son, Simba, was living in the United Kingdom at this time, and he offered to have her come and live with him. "I wanted to go to my son," Susan admitted, "but I knew if I went anywhere other than the refugee camps I would not find peace." So Susan made the decision to go to the camps at Adjumani and find children to help.

It was 1994 when Susan made her journey to the Adjumani refugee camps in Northern Uganda. Small round tukuls (huts) with thatched roofs were scattered all around the ramshackle town, interspersed with jumbled together storefront-type buildings. During the late 1980's, 85,000 Sudanese refugees had fled across the Nile to Uganda to escape the civil war in Sudan. They overwhelmed the small town of 20,000 people. By the time Susan arrived, all the refugees were still there as the war in Sudan raged on. They had been placed in crowded refugee camps. The resources were meager. The security was non-existent.

As Susan came to the Adjumani refugee camps, she saw first hand how the children were suffering. "The need was overwhelming," she remembers. Susan began making her way around the town, looking for children. There was a long row of trees down each side of the one main street. The British had planted them in earlier colonial times. There was a long deep trench on each side of the street that contained debris and garbage that was being burned with small fires. People lined the street, many selling small piles of fruit or various trinkets.

There were trees and bushes scattered among the tukuls on the outskirts of town, some of them partially cut down to use for firewood. One day as she was passing by a bush she heard crying.

She had found her first child – a toddler named Victoria.

Susan found out that Victoria had lost her mother a day after birth. The father was young and afraid, and had simply disappeared. There was an old widow who tried to take care of Victoria, but she had fallen ill herself. Victoria was little more than a skeleton. She was about two years old and unable to sit up on her own. She sometimes ate feces because there was nothing else to eat. Susan brought the child to where she was staying.

After just a week, Victoria started to walk and smile at people. Susan decided to rent a tukul, and lived in it with Victoria. Many people started to come to Susan with other children as they learned of her work. She had to look elsewhere for help in caring for the children since she lived among refugees who were struggling for their own survival.

Susan began to sell gold bangles and clothing in Kampala, the capital city of Uganda. She was able to purchase one tukul from the elders of Adjumani. The tukul became too small as people began to bring her many more children. Susan's sister, Naomi, continued to send money. Susan scraped by, and was able to increase the tukuls to two.

The Netherlands Embassy gifted her $9,000, and the United Nations gave her additional aid after a friend helped her write some grants. The tukuls increased. The children continued to come. More clothing was purchased. Beds, medicine, and mosquito nets were obtained.

Just as Susan's vision was beginning to move forward, it was suddenly derailed. The UN decided that refugees who lived in the Oligi transit camp (where she was) must be transferred to other settlement camps within the Adjumani and Moyo Districts.

Susan recalls: "We were relocated to the Maaji settlement, which is very far from the town of Adjumani. The LRA used to stay near that camp, and many refugees were killed in that settlement. We therefore refused to go." (The LRA, Lord's Resistance Army, is a notorious rebel group known for kidnapping children and forcing them to become child soldiers and sex slaves.)

The situation intensified when the UN's staff came very early one morning and ordered Susan and the children to get their belongings out of the tukuls. Susan refused. Shockingly, all their belongings were thrown out of the tukuls by people they were told had been hired by the UN. The buildings were then destroyed within a few hours.

"We wept and the children wept," Susan remembers. "We were left up in the air again without shelter. Our local pastors came to pray for us. Some of them agreed to take some children into their families temporarily."

A friend of Susan's from France heard about their situation. He traveled to Uganda to confirm what had happened. He then returned to France and told the news to the pupils of St. Just College. Susan explains, "The children, mostly ages nine to twelve, agreed with their teachers to organize a race to raise funds. They raised enough money for me to buy some land in Adjumani, build some tukuls, and eventually bring the children back home." To Susan, it was a demonstration of God's grace to have the children's home reborn. She named the new orphanage "Amazing Grace Children's Home."

At the critical point when Susan decided to follow the dreams she had years earlier, she became like Moses: "… choosing rather to suffer affliction with the people of God than to enjoy the passing pleasures of sin, esteeming the reproach of Christ greater riches than the treasures in Egypt; for he looked to the reward." (Hebrews 11:25-26). Ever since those humble and chaotic beginnings, "she extends her hand to the poor, yes, she reaches out her hands to the needy." (Proverbs 31:20).

Mama Susan bathing one of the first children she took in

13

Mama Susan Tabia

2

FIRST ENCOUNTER
Kampala, Uganda

My first step on African soil was at Entebbe Airport in Kampala, Uganda. The other travelers and I stepped off the plane and down a long staircase onto the tarmac. Floodlights rimmed the perimeter and the air was hot and humid. Tropical vegetation, odors, and sounds bombarded our senses. We shed layers of clothing to cool off as we came down the steps, and prepared for the long wait to get through customs.

I traveled with a group of young people, led by Dan Holcomb of Lahash International. As a retired nurse, I didn't know if I could keep up with this energetic group but they kindly allowed me to travel with them. I first heard about Dan's work through his parents, Ron and Char Holcomb, who had been missionaries in Sudan and Kenya for many years.

Lahash is a Hebrew word meaning "whispered prayer." The organization's name was chosen as a reminder of those who are so weak that all they can do is whisper a prayer. Dan saw people in that situation and wanted to help. He had started Lahash a couple years before, when he met Mama Susan in Northern Uganda and she wanted him to publicize the needs of her orphans.

Dan's vision was to partner Christian ministries in East Africa with those in the West who wanted to help. Susan was the first East African Lahash partner. Our first stops on a four country tour would be to visit her projects in Uganda and Sudan.

Our plane was late that night, and it was about two a.m. when I first met Mama Susan. She had come with a local volunteer to pick us up. She was wearing traditional African attire, and seemed very quiet and unassuming. At that time I hadn't heard about her life. I only knew that everyone seemed to admire and respect her very much.

Our conversation was minimal as we piled into the van with our multitude of trunks. Everyone was fatigued. Although she speaks seven languages, including English, Mama Susan is essentially deaf, which makes conversation difficult. When we spoke to her, her assistant spoke right into her ear in her native language and then she replied to us in English.

We each carried two fifty-pound trunks of supplies for the orphanages, including lots of medical supplies. Dan wanted us to be as mobile as possible on the trip, and to bring as much for the children as we could. He asked that we carry the entirety of our personal items in a backpack for our five-week journey.

As we climbed into the van and drove down the highway from the airport to Kampala, I looked at all the flickering lights along the way and wondered about what might be in store over the next few weeks in Uganda and Sudan. We would be visiting the Amazing Grace Children's Home in Uganda, and then crossing the Nile to the other orphanage she had since developed in Sudan – St.

Bartholomew's. We would also visit her other projects for widows and people with leprosy.

It was about a forty-five minute drive to Susan's house. When we arrived at her neighborhood, the van started shaking violently as it made its way down the hill to her house. The roadway was rutted with deep grooves, some two or three feet deep. The van twisted and swayed side to side and dipped down into the deep holes. It was amazing. I had never been on such a road, but we made it to the house and piled out of the van, Susan leading the way.

We carried the trunks into her very small house and piled them up. I couldn't help but notice that in one room there was a line of kids, probably ten or so, sleeping on the floor. They were on their sides and looked like cord-wood all lined up in a row. I was amazed that they could sleep in such a small space and in such a straight row.

That was my first inkling that Mama Susan was a woman of great faith and courage. She took such a large group of children into her own home, on top of all her other responsibilities. It made me want to know more about her, and I looked forward to what was in store on the journey ahead.

Children sleeping at Mama Susan's

The busy streets of Kampala

3

KAMPALA
Capital City and Susan's Home

"Sing, O barren, you who have not borne! Break forth into singing, and cry aloud, you who have not labored with child! For more are the children of the desolate than the children of the married woman," says the Lord. – Isaiah 54:1

Kampala, Uganda, is a large and sprawling city – a mixture of new and old, broken sidewalks and beautiful vistas. We were to stay at an Episcopal girls' school. We arrived so late at night that we just had time to wash in a basin and sink into bed.

When we first awoke, we could see the greenery of the yards and tile roofs as we looked out from the second floor balcony. There were lovely birds singing, and beautiful tropical trees and flowers framed the grounds.

Breakfast was served European style in the dining room, where the girls also ate. Our tables were ready with cereal, milk, tea, toast and jam. There were even some hard-boiled eggs and peanut butter for protein.

Most of the time in Kampala we traveled by boda

boda, a little motorbike that would zoom around town, in and out between cars. It was a fun ride, but of course no one had helmets. When all five or six of us traveled together, the drivers would race to catch up or out-maneuver each other, daring to see how close to the cars they could get.

While staying with Mama Susan that week, I realized the boda boda was also her primary way to travel in town. It must have been hard for her to travel at times, as she was often carrying food from the markets or other heavy parcels for her projects. I knew she used the boda boda because she couldn't afford a taxi or car.

The first night in Kampala, we went to Mama Susan's for dinner. When she wasn't on the road supervising her various projects, she had a home in the city to maintain close access to resources for her children. When we arrived, her children were waiting for us, sitting on large mats by her little house. She and the older children prepared dinner outdoors on a low charcoal grill. We had a lot of time to sit and visit with the children. The children next door were singing songs on their back porch. Soon, we were all dancing around the yard, singing and playing together with the children.

Mama Susan had just taken in one little orphan who was nothing but skin and bones. We couldn't believe how thin and frail she was, thinking she must have looked like Mama's first child, Victoria.

After supper the children sat on a mat in the living room and sang and prayed together. Their worship and prayers were quite lovely and touching. I was surprised by their joy. It was obvious they did it with their whole hearts.

The children worked constantly to help with cooking and other chores. They would wash all the clothes in little pans outside and hang them on the line to dry. They were happy, in what most would consider very hard times. They had no toys, hardly any clothes, sometimes not enough food, but always smiles and laughter.

I thought of two scriptures as I reflected on how happy the children were, even in their situation: Nehemiah 8:10, "...for the joy of the Lord is your strength," and Jesus' words in Luke 6:20, "Blessed are you poor, for yours is the kingdom of God."

Dan Holcomb, director of Lahash International, with the children outside Susan's home in Kampala

Amazing Grace Children's Home

4

TRAVELING NORTH
Amazing Grace Children's Home
in Adjumani, Uganda

We waited in Kampala to get our visas for Sudan. Then we traveled to the Amazing Grace Children's Home in northern Uganda to spend a few days before continuing to St. Bartholomew's in Sudan.

Susan's vision had been first to find orphans in the Adjumani refugee camps. It later grew to include the war-torn region of Kajo Keji in Southern Sudan, where she had opened St. Bartholomew's Children's Home a few years later. She had visited and seen that the children there were suffering even more than those she had found in Adjumani. Many of the orphans there had witnessed the deaths of their parents and siblings.

The Episcopal Church of Sudan gave Susan some land in Kajo Keji. Many international friends and organizations, as well as her Sudanese and Ugandan friends helped her raise funds and build tukuls. Others gave her clothes. Now St. Bartholomew's had grown to become home for sixty Sudanese orphans.

Our plan was to take the Sudanese war orphans

from Amazing Grace with us across the Nile to celebrate Christmas with the children at St. Bartholomew's. It was going to be a great adventure as many of the children from Amazing Grace hadn't seen their relatives or been to their home country of Sudan for many years. We looked forward to being a part of that homecoming for these dear children. (Susan has kept Amazing Grace open in case war breaks out in Sudan again and she needs a place to relocate the children of St. Bartholomew's.)

Our van was bulging with travelers and baggage as we drove to Adjumani. It was a sunny day and we looked forward to seeing the countryside and to meeting the children. The eight-hour trip was uneventful. We arrived at the Amazing Grace compound later that day. We were happy to see all thirty children waiting for us with their big smiles.

Mama Susan brought a cook to help the regular orphanage cooks. They had to sit or squat next to the cooking fires that burned with wooden charcoal briquettes. The children helped with the cooking, and especially with giving out the food and washing the dishes. The kids would bring water for the orphanage in heavy yellow "jerry cans" from a nearby pump. Susan made sure that we travelers had bottled water.

Later that evening the children were outside dancing in the dark with the Lahash travelers (who had brought flashlights and battery-powered music). I decided I wanted to discuss some medical plans for the children with Mama Susan. By then it was about 9:30 p.m. and the ladies let me go into her tukul. There she was, at the end of a long day, sorting through piles of paper work. Her work still was not done, but she was gracious and kind to take time to consult with me. She reminded me of the woman in Proverbs 31:18 whose "lamp does not go out by night."

Susan constantly struggles with getting enough funds to feed, clothe, and pay school fees for all the children in her care. She does get some help, but it is not enough to cover all the needs. When we saw the orphans at Amazing Grace we were a little shocked. Most of them had threadbare clothing, and their medical needs were obvious.

Many of them had open cuts and sores that had never been cleaned or bandaged. A lot of them had some type of fungal rash on their heads. We had some medical supplies with us and were able to treat and take care of several of the health issues. We took some of the children with more serious needs into town to the medical clinic to be treated.

The children played and entertained themselves for hours during the day. They didn't really have much except a partially inflated soccer ball or some broken toys. I remember bringing a coloring book and giving the kids each one page to color. They were so grateful and spent about two hours not moving from their spots, carefully and creatively coloring the pages that they were given.

The sky at the Amazing Grace Children's Home was dramatic, and each night there was a beautiful sunset. There was a huge tree on the orphanage grounds. Its branches were spread like a hovering giant, watching over the children as they slept. I was struck by the overwhelming beauty of the place, including the silhouette of that large tree.

Another time I was awed by the sky was at bath time. The starry expanse was our ceiling. There was a small cement enclosure into which the girls would bring plastic buckets of water that they had warmed over the fire. We took turns bathing under the stars in the moonlight as we prepared ourselves for sleep.

I was a little surprised to learn that the orphanage had a night watchman who stayed awake all night with his bow and arrow ready, continuously surveying the grounds in case he had to protect the children and staff.

Our mission on this trip was a joyful one, and it was exciting to think of taking these thirty children who were refugees of war on an adventure across the Nile to visit their homeland of Sudan for Christmas.

The children were very excited the day we rose early to begin our trek to Sudan. We had a huge lorry (truck) to carry the thirty children. It was piled high with luggage and packages. They didn't have any real suitcases, but large plastic bags and bins and many containers most likely left by other travelers. Children sat and stood on top of the "luggage" jammed together in the open-air truck. There were no such things as helmets, seat belts, or enclosed roofs.

Mama Susan and the cooks had been up almost all night preparing food for us to take on our journey. Again I was reminded of scripture: "She also rises while it is yet night, and provides food for her household." (Proverbs 31:15).

The workers and young Lahash travelers climbed in the back with the children. I was given the honor, as a senior citizen, to ride in the cab of the truck with Mama Susan and her sister, Judith. Judith was seated in the crawlspace behind our seat, which was about 18 inches wide. We were packed in between and underneath all sorts of bags and packages. It was quite a project to un-wrap ourselves. We had to move all the packages off our laps and from all around us in order to get out whenever the lorry stopped.

Our travels would take us over unpaved gravel and increasingly rough and rutted roads from Northern Uganda, across the Nile, and then about forty miles into the southernmost part of Sudan to St. Bartholomew's.

Piling in the lorry to head into Sudan

Lyla and the group heading into Sudan

5

WAR
Up Close and Personal

It was with excitement and a little bit of fear that I thought about traveling into Sudan. As we began traveling along the rough and rutted roads, my thoughts went to some of the things I had heard about Sudan and about Susan.

I first heard about Sudan in the mid-1990's when the organization Voice of the Martyrs asked people to send blankets to the people of South Sudan. The country was in the middle of a brutal civil war. The mostly Muslim North wanted to impose Shari'ah Law on the mostly Christian South. Reports were that over two million South Sudanese died and several million were displaced as the well-armed North relentlessly bombed the South. Many people were sleeping outside with no covering and were suffering in many ways.

Also in the mid-90's, many people in U.S. churches were talking about the slave trade in Sudan. "Slavers" from the north would come and capture Southerners. Some churches sent donations in the $50 increments required to redeem slaves, and others felt that this was wrong and that it would encourage more slavery.

I met a mission executive about this time who told me that activists were wondering why more Christians weren't speaking out and trying to help their brothers and sisters in Sudan. I didn't do anything about it at the time, but it established Sudan in my mind as a place where horrible things were happening.

I also thought about Susan and the things she had suffered. She had talked about the fact that when she was a teenager, she lived in the middle of the civil war that raged within her own home and throughout her home town of Yambio, Sudan. She relates that her fellow Sudanese would come into her family's home screaming and hiding under their beds to dodge the bullets. Her father was killed during that time. I simply could not imagine what that would be like – a brutal war coming as close as my own home and family.

She again experienced war up close and personal when she returned to Sudan as a young woman, after the death of her husband in the United Kingdom. She was very depressed, and her friends talked her into going back to Juba, where they had the family home. She recounts that the civil war had intensified and the violence was even worse than what she previously had seen. She said people would dig holes, called khandahs, to hide from the bombs in a desperate attempt to shield themselves. Often, they would still be killed. She would see orphans standing outside hospitals with no one helping them. Her heart went out to the children as they looked so frail and desolate in their ragged clothing.

As Sudan became a place of increasing terror and violence, a doctor's note became her ticket to leave. He wrote that she needed better medical access to treat her hypertension, a heart irregularity, and malaria. She took her small son, Simba, and moved to Kenya. It was years later that she returned to Uganda, to the Adjumani refugee camps, and started gathering Sudanese war orphans.

These stories reminded me of the heroes of faith mentioned in Hebrews 11:37b-38, who "wandered about in sheepskins and goatskins, being destitute, afflicted, tormented -- of whom the world was not worthy. They wandered in deserts and mountains, in dens and caves of the earth." It also brought to mind I Peter 1:6-7, "...now for a little while, if need be, you have been grieved by various trials, that the genuineness of your faith, being much more precious than gold that perishes, though it is tested by fire, may be found to praise, honor, and glory at the revelation of Jesus Christ..."

As we continued our journey to Sudan, I thought of these things. I realized that the people of Sudan had suffered so much, yet their love for their land was very deep. I began to wonder: "What will Sudan look like? What will the people be like? How will the Amazing Grace children respond to seeing their homeland and family and friends after all these years?" These thoughts and questions flooded my mind as we made our slow and bumpy way along the rutted road to Sudan. But we would first have to cross the Nile River.

Waiting for the ferry on the banks of the Nile

6

CROSSING THE NILE
Bringing the Sudanese War Orphans
Home to Visit Sudan

When we got to the Nile River, there was a ferry dock and all kinds of people milling around. The simply constructed dock was made of wood and steel. It looked too small for our truck and all the others, but we made it. That day, we got right across, but other times we would wait hours for our turn or for repairs to be made.

We had traveled about twenty miles after crossing the Nile when we came to the sign and gate telling us we were entering Sudan. It was hard to believe we were really in Sudan. The entrance to the country had a simple farm-type gate and a few soldiers guarding it. We pulled over to have our papers checked and were soon on our way up the road.

The countryside was lovely. There were wide expanses of grasslands dotted with large trees, many of them mango trees. I could see why the people loved this land. It was truly a land of beauty.

The lorry suddenly came to a halt as we were traveling. It had stopped by a large mango tree where a small group of people were sitting by the side of the road. The excitement of the children was at a peak as they saw Mama Susan get out of the lorry and negotiate with the sellers for some of the fresh fruit. Sudan is known for its mangoes and it had been several years since the children had been able to eat one. They ate with great enjoyment and I thought it must have added to their sense of coming home.

Mama Susan, due to her hearing problems, didn't talk much on the ride. Also, the road was so rough and noisy, it was difficult to think. There are only forty miles of paved road in South Sudan, which is as large as the state of Texas. The roads have been washed out in the rainy seasons and never repaired. The truck felt like it was riding on the ocean with huge waves. It would dip down into a three-foot hole and then up and out, preparing to dip down again for the next one. It was a wild ride.

It took us two or three hours to travel the thirty or forty miles to the children's home in Kajo Keji. The home was set in the rolling hills about half a mile from town. The sun was shining and the wind lightly blowing over the grassy hillsides. The children were waiting for us, and as we approached they began to sing a welcoming song. It was an emotional time, especially for all the children on the lorry who were "coming home."

St. Bartholomew's Children's Home looked attractive, dotted with several tukuls. It seemed like arriving at a place that one just reads about in books or sees on a travel show. It felt remote and untouched, like a special destination where one would go to get away and be refreshed and renewed.

That first night in Sudan was full of excitement as the children from Amazing Grace Children's Home found places to sleep. Some ended up in the tents that had been packed, and others crowded in with the children who were already there. The children settled to enjoy their homeland, laughing and talking together and obviously very happy.

Susan was very much the lady in charge, with her quiet authority. A steady stream of workers, cooks, and children were coming to help her as she organized meals, had supplies unloaded, and assigned children their places to sleep.

One of Susan's workers was a most hospitable and friendly man. He was fluent in English and carried out Susan's wishes efficiently. They seemed to work well together in managing all the details and logistics of combining the two orphanages for the week.

We were finally settling in Sudan – a land that had seen much tragedy, but also a beautiful land that was home to all these dear children. It was going to be interesting to see what the week would bring forth, and I felt a great sense of joy to be there and be able to witness the event of the children's reunion with their land, a land I had heard so much about.

The border crossing into Sudan

Children in Sudan around a battery-powered Christmas tree

7

CHRISTMAS IN SUDAN
A Time to Remember

"You may not be able to change the whole world,
but you can change the world for one child."
- Wess Stafford, Compassion International

That Christmas Eve is very strongly embedded in my mind. We were all homesick, and I remember acutely missing my family and wondering why I was in Sudan instead of home with them. We had done some good things during our stay, but Christmas Eve was a time for grandmas to be with their grandkids. Some of the other team members were especially homesick that night as well.

The kids were singing and dancing in the lamplight. It was fun to watch, but we were tired and just wanted to be with our families. With half of my thoughts at home, I wandered inside a big tent that had been set up outside. I saw a little girl standing by the inner tent post. Her head was shaved bald, just like all the other kids, and was covered with some of the white ointment we had applied for the fungus. She was barefoot, wearing a frilly dress that was very torn and dirty. She was crying, so I asked a person standing near her to find out what was wrong. Why was the little girl crying?

Her answer was, "Soil in my eye and a headache." My roommate and I took the little girl into our tukul, which had a better lantern for light. One of the team members had some Murine, so we borrowed that and washed out her eye. We also gave her a bottle of water and a baby aspirin. Later that night we saw her again and she looked much happier. The next day she was laughing and playing with the others.

After helping the little girl, Juru, I cried really hard. The reality was that this little girl didn't even know she could ask anyone for help. Here she was on Christmas Eve, suffering in silence, a single frail girl in a ragged dress with soil in her eye and a headache. It seemed like all the suffering, need, and lack of resources around us were wrapped up in that one little girl. It made me realize the greatness of the work of Mama Susan: a woman who came with no resources, reaching out in faith to do what she could to help these children. I could see it was a place where each thing, no matter how small or large, means so much in the life of a child.

During our first two days there, the children quickly got to know one another and had hours of fun, talking and laughing and playing soccer. Those who had family in the area were reunited with them.

We had been busy with the medical needs of both children and staff. We spent a lot of time cleaning wounds, putting on bandages, and giving simple first aid. We took four or five of the children with more severe health problems, like asthma or ear infections, into town for treatment in the local clinic.

We had just two days to prepare for Christmas. We were planning a big Christmas party for the neighborhood. The children made artwork from supplies we brought with us. The finished products were strung around the edges of a large tent. One traveler had also brought a small battery-powered Christmas tree that we set up on a chair in the evenings. This was probably the first Christmas tree any of them had seen.

There was no electricity or running water, but the children would bring water from a well at the edge of the property. A generator was run for a few hours at night for lights. Two staff members put up a makeshift screen that they were able to use to show the children a movie one night, using a generator-powered device. That was a huge treat for everyone! It was amazing to see how overjoyed they were to see things that Americans take for granted!

Christmas Day dawned, and some of the young travelers went out to watch a cow being butchered. It would provide a Christmas feast for the orphanage, the neighborhood, and visiting pastors and dignitaries from Kajo Keji.

The children rarely had meat to eat, perhaps once a year. Their main staples are a kind of corn meal porridge or rice. Sometimes they are fortunate enough to have mangoes, or peanuts from the peanut farm at Amazing Grace. The orphanage did have some cows in a pasture a few miles away, but they were all so skinny that it looked like they would provide very little to eat. They were rarely used for food, but were like long term insurance in case even harder times should come.

The great turnout for the Christmas dinner and the kind words of many guests were a measure of Mama Susan's stature in the community. The chief of police, various pastors, and other leaders were in attendance. Mama Susan gave a speech, and our team gave a few words to the assembled crowd as well.

We had cooked large pots of rice for the meal. I sat on the mat with the children. I noticed that their entire Christmas meal consisted solely of the rice, a few bites of meat, and a soda (which we had provided for them). That is all they had to eat. But they appeared to be content and excited with the food and all the festivities.

Later, Dan had us bring bowls of water to the dining tukul. He had the children and staff line up and come in. We knelt beside each one and washed their feet. I felt so privileged to wash Mama Susan's feet, this woman who "watches over the ways of her household, and does not eat the bread of idleness." (Proverbs 31:27). My roommate washed the feet of Susan's sister, Judith. By this time, I had seen the huge responsibility Mama carried, the vast number of people she had to care for, and the grace and dignity with which she carried herself. Here, more than anywhere else, there was a stream of people in and out of her tukul seeking advice, direction, and assistance from early morning until well into the night.

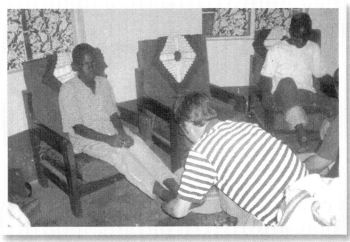

The Lahash team washing the feet of children and staff at St. Bartholomew's

8

COMPASSIONATE OUTREACH
People with Leprosy and Others in Distress

"Blessed be… the God of all comfort, who comforts us in all our tribulation, that we may be able to comfort those who are in any trouble, with the comfort with which we ourselves are comforted by God. For as the sufferings of Christ abound in us, so our consolation also abounds through Christ."
– II Corinthians 1:3-5

"My boy, my boy!" The young woman half screamed as she paced back and forth in great grief. Mama Susan was next to her, with tears rolling down her face, trying to speak words of comfort. We had driven up to a large farm and entered the yard to find the woman pacing back and forth. Mama immediately went to her side.

The young woman had just buried her four-year-old son. He had been run over by a tractor. A guest had given the boy a ride, and he had fallen off, under the tractor. The young woman was inconsolable. Mama Susan was grieving with her and doing her best to comfort her. There was a little bed out in the field where they had kept his body, and had just buried him that day. There were people seated around the yard in chairs who had also come to comfort the couple.

This incident was another example of Mama Susan's tireless compassion. We encountered the grieving mother on our way back to St. Bartholomew's after visiting the town of Magiri about ten miles north. Our purpose there was to visit yet another group that Mama Susan had been working to help: people afflicted with leprosy.

Susan did her best to tell others of the needs of the people with leprosy and to bring them food and clothing whenever she could. She would take visitors to see them and they would come back with food. Lahash had been able to raise funds to purchase a lot of food and medical supplies, which we delivered.

A large number of the people with leprosy returned to Sudan from refugee camps in Uganda because of the peace agreement that was signed between North and South Sudan in 2005. A retired Episcopal priest (a friend of Susan's and the father of one of her workers) had a church there for the people.

Leprosy was something I had heard of from the Bible, but had never seen as a nurse. In fact, I was surprised to find out people still had this disease. When we got to Magiri, many people had made their way to wait for us under a tree. They eagerly awaited our arrival. It was touching to see people of various ages, some with problems walking or missing fingers and/or toes, who had somehow managed to get there to meet us.

We decided to do some interviews with the help of an interpreter. We hoped by doing the interviews we might help them get the needed medication by documenting some of their cases. The people had such a great desire to get medication for treatment. There are some antibiotics that can treat leprosy so that they are no longer contagious. They could then live back with others in the community.

Many of the people had been partially treated in refugee camps, but some had received no treatment. We were shocked to find that some children, often children of parents who had leprosy, were beginning to show signs of the disease. Sadly, due to lack of medical access and instability in the region, the people do not have the medications even to this day.

One man especially touched our hearts as he asked for a simple pair of gloves for his wife, because she had to crawl on the ground to care for their three children.

We felt we didn't have a lot to offer, but what we had was accepted with joy and gratefulness. We sang, danced, left supplies, prayed with the people, and then left to go back to the children's home.

Soon, we were back to St. Bartholomew's for a few days. One of the projects Mama Susan had for us was to make some home visits to people in the community near the orphanage. We also visited a retired Episcopal bishop, who was a personal friend of Susan's and had also married her and her husband.

Our first community visit was to a woman with leprosy who lived with her daughter-in-law in ramshackle housing. She had serious foot wounds that we were able to dress with bandages. We left her with some dressing supplies. She was unable to leave the family compound to go anywhere in the community because she couldn't walk. Another visit was to a blind grandmother, struggling to feed her grandchildren. We took food, soap, and other gifts to them.

A few days later we made the journey with the Amazing Grace children back over the Nile to Uganda. We travelers continued with Mama Susan to her home in Kampala.

We were impressed that Susan reached out beyond her own projects to others in the community with a wide range of needs: people with leprosy, those in grief, those in authority, and those with other needs. Mama Susan reached out and ministered to all those around.

Mama Susan gives a blanket to a woman with leprosy

9

WIDOWS AND FAIR TRADE
Overcoming Personal Tragedy

"Pure and undefiled religion before God and the Father is this: to visit orphans and widows in their trouble…" – James 1:27

It was through the writings of other travelers that I heard the story of how Susan became a widow and the terrible grief and depression she suffered after losing her husband. It is clear that she was able to draw something from that difficult experience, and to reach out and help others in similar situations, even with her limited resources.

Susan and her husband were newly married and living in the United Kingdom where he studied for his masters degree. They had lived there for two years, and he had just been accepted into a Ph.D. program in the United States. She and her friends had gathered together for a party to celebrate, but he never came. They waited and waited until 4:00 a.m., when a police officer knocked on the door. A train had crushed her beloved husband, Eliakin Gubang. Their son, Simba, was just twenty-five days old.

Susan was distraught, almost suicidal, after her husband's death. Her friends advised her to return to the family home in Juba, Sudan. She agreed, but said even after she returned and lived among other Christians she had no peace.

Then one night, she was given a vision while half asleep. People were singing joyfully in the air between the sky and the earth, "Jesus gives peace, good peace to us. The world looks beautiful because we believe in Him." She saw Jesus standing above them in the air. She remembers, "I woke up and started singing. From that time on, I found true peace. I accepted my situation and stuck to Jesus, the author of peace."

Susan founded an organization called IWASSRU (International Widow's Association of South Sudanese Refugees in Uganda) in 1994, around the same time that she started gathering orphans. Thousands of widows fled to Uganda from the war in Sudan, and Susan admits that it was her own experience as a widow trying to support an infant son that led her to form this 500-member organization.

Under Susan's leadership, IWASSRU manages all the orphanages and other community projects. They have also developed a fair trade group which trains widows to sew, tailor, and market their hand-crafted products.

On Christmas Day at St. Bartholomew's, Susan had presented each of the team members with an item of African clothing, a dress or shirt that had been produced by IWASSRU. She had selected just the right one for each of us, the perfect color and size. The fabrics were vivid and beautiful.

When we arrived back at her home in Kampala, Susan laid out many lovely baskets, beautiful tie-dyed and batik clothing, and other items she had for sale. We were amazed at the craftsmanship they displayed. All these goods had been produced by widows in difficult circumstances.

By the time we left Susan's home to continue our journey, our trunks were packed with clothing and baskets that the widows had made. Knowing that the funds would go to help the widows gave us extra incentive to purchase extra items. We bought many items for gifts and also took some that we would try to sell at home.

As we got in the van to leave Susan, my heart was thankful for all we had seen and learned. As beautiful as the handmade garments were, I could truly say of Susan that "strength and honor are her clothing." (Proverbs 31:25).

On a later trip to Africa, I was able to travel with Susan to one of the sites where the baskets are made, and I watched her inspect and purchase sixty baskets. We took them to her home, where workers packaged them and mailed them to a customer.

She markets many of the widows' items on the internet though SERRV and agreatergift.com.

Mama Susan inspecting baskets

St. Bartholomew's Children's Home in southern Sudan

10

TERROR BY NIGHT
A Fear-Filled Week in Sudan

"You shall not be afraid of the terror by night,
nor of the arrow that flies by day..."
- Psalm 91:5

After that first trip to Sudan in 2006, I was very motivated to return. I traveled a few months later to a leprosy conference in Uganda. Then in February 2008, I revisited all the orphanages. I was amazed to see all the improvements that the advocacy of Dan Holcomb and Lahash had generated. One young man with a love for the Lord and for East Africa had brought in support from all over the world through the Lahash website.

It was wonderful to see all the progress that had been made in just one year. There were several volunteers that came to help after being touched by the Lahash message. I was able to spend time with two of them on this second visit to St. Bartholomew's, José Nunez from California, and Ashley Eggert from Port Angeles, Washington.

I wasn't prepared for the events of one frightful week during this trip to St. Bartholomew's. Ashley, José, and I had been studying Ephesians 3 together by lantern light, and then we finished with prayer. They had been at the orphanage for several months. It was nearing midnight, and we could hear the beginning of a windstorm outside. We decided to head to bed. We were feeling a little apprehensive because we had been hearing reports that the Lord's Resistance Army (LRA) had just abducted 22 women and children from Magiri, about ten miles away.

I had heard about the LRA before, at home and from others in Africa. I knew they had no mercy, even forcing children to kill their own parents. Other times they would slice off noses, ears, lips, and limbs if the children weren't able to carry the heavy loads of supplies assigned to them.

As I left the dining room tukul and headed to the outdoor latrine, my fear increased as I wondered if any LRA were nearby. The orphanage is about a half mile out of town and is in a hilly, grassy area, leaving it exposed with no place to hide. I had a flashlight, but I purposely left it off because I didn't want to draw any attention. The wind was literally howling, gaining momentum. Pieces of branches flew from the few small trees and the buildings were creaking in the wind. I peered into the darkness, watching for any signs of the LRA.

Finally, I made it back to the sleeping tukul, which was hot and humid despite the windstorm. The tukul was round with a thatched roof, cement floor, wooden shutters, and a wooden door. I shut the door tightly behind me, but my hands were shaking so hard it was difficult to close the window shutters.

Lying down on the thin mat to sleep, I was conscious of the volume and intensity of the wind, and I also began to hear people yelling and screaming. My heart sank as I thought, "Dear Lord, this is it. They are coming here to capture us!" I was paralyzed with fear, lying in bed, listening and praying. My thoughts were rambling, thinking, "What would I do if attacked?" There was no bed or furniture to hide under. I tried to picture myself going out to stand in front of the children's dorms, faced by maniacs with machine guns. I realized it wasn't in me to do it. All I could think of was my family and the grandchildren I wanted to see grow up. I realized how vulnerable we were. There was no way to escape.

That was the beginning of a harrowing week with the same type of fear at bedtime each night. Ashley and I went into town to the UN headquarters and learned that they were on high alert. We also went to the hospital and talked to an intern named Dr. J. from Sierra Leone. She and the head nurse had their bags packed beside their beds in case they had to flee at night. She said a young woman had walked into town with a suitcase on her head, stating that her husband had been killed by the LRA in the attack near Magiri.

Dr. J. said she had heard word that officials were sending more soldiers for protection, but all week I never saw one on duty, or even walking around the town. I didn't see any police on duty either, even though I looked for them every day.

We talked to a local who said that people had fled into the bush the night before and they thought the LRA was about two miles west of town. Three suspects who were strangers in town were arrested. It appeared they were "casing out" the area.

One morning I told José how afraid I was. I had just spent another sleepless night feeling particularly fearful, lying awake in a cold sweat with my heart pounding wildly. José said, "Where is your faith?" I thought about that for a long time. Where was my faith?

I had always hoped that if I had to suffer for Christ, I would never deny Him and would stand strong. But I had to be honest and admit that I didn't want to try to protect the orphans or take any risks. I just wanted to go home. I was able to return home after a week, but Ashley and José stayed at the orphanage for several more months. Their faith, and that of Mama Susan, amazed me.

Susan told me about a terrifying experience she and the Amazing Grace children had with the LRA in 2004. The LRA entered the Adjumani Catholic Mission, which is very close to Amazing Grace. They captured some orphans from there, most of whom were Sudanese. Four of them were hacked to death because they were not strong enough to walk long distances with luggage on their heads.

Susan told me that the LRA threatened that their next target was Amazing Grace. Some of the male staff panicked and wanted to close the orphanage. But Susan prayed scripture out loud:

"Do not fear, for those who are with us are more than those who are with them." (II Kings 6:16).

"Be strong and courageous; do not be afraid nor dismayed before the king of Assyria, nor before all the multitude that is with him; for there are more with us than with him. With him is an arm of flesh; but with us is the Lord our God, to help us and to fight our battles." (II Chronicles 32:7-8).

She read I John 4:4 to the children: "You are of God, little children, and have overcome them, because He who is in you is greater than he who is in the world."

Susan and the staff decided to stay and keep the orphanage open. "Fortunately no rebels came near Amazing Grace," she said, "although they used to pass by. Praise God." I finally understood why there was a watchman at the Amazing Grace Children's Home.

As I reflected on all of this, I had a new awareness of the fear Mama Susan faced many times in her life due to her personal exposure to years of war and terror. She faced it in both Sudan and Uganda, and there is a high probability she will have to face it again. Hebrews 11:33-34 describes her journey: "...through faith worked righteousness, obtained promises... quenched the violence of fire, escaped the edge of the sword, out of weakness were made strong, became valiant in battle, turned to flight the armies of the aliens."

The fear I felt during that week at St. Bartholomew's gave me a whole new appreciation of Susan's courage and faith. After years of living through the terrors of war, she is still there to aid, comfort, and care for her orphans. It made me want to share her story so others could understand the courageous choices she has made.

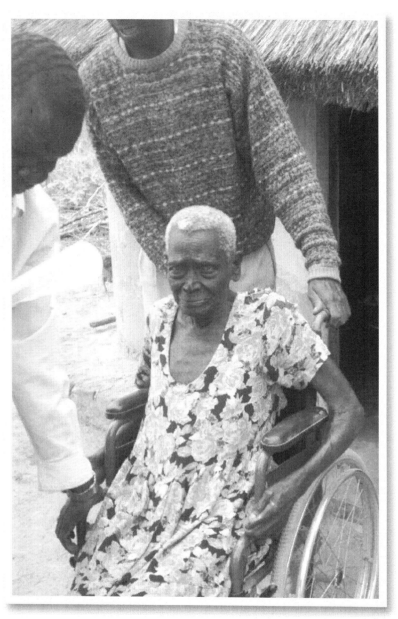

A donated wheelchair provides mobility for a widow with leprosy

11

BRIDGING THE GAP
Face to Face and Online

"Lahash International partners with East
Africans, advocating and caring for the
vulnerable in response to Christ's love."
– Lahash Mission Statement

That fearful week definitely affected my visit. It made me aware of my shortcomings in faith, as well as the very real dangers that surround the orphanages. In spite of that, I was very pleased to see all the progress that had been made on Susan's various projects and in the lives of those under her care.

When I visited Susan's home again, the frail little child she had taken in back in 2006 had gained weight and was happily running around and playing, looking much healthier and stronger.

A man in Great Britain learned through the Lahash website that Mama Susan had a vision for a home for babies at St. Bartholomew's in Sudan. He decided to fund it. By the time of my 2008 trip, the baby facility had been constructed, as well as new dorms for the children and a training center for sewing.

At my return to St. Bartholomew's, Juru was the first child I looked for. I was happy to see her doing well. I was even able to walk to church with her and Ashley, the long-term volunteer. I took some photos of Juru dancing with her friends.

The orphanage had a nurse on duty and a medical dispensary thanks to the work of Lahash and other volunteers and donors. I was able to bring several donations with me. I brought scales, medicines, clothing, mosquito nets, and a solar microscope to help diagnose malaria. A wheelchair had already been sent for the woman with leprosy who had to crawl on the ground, and I brought several pairs of gloves for her and others like her.

The other woman with leprosy who lived near the orphanage also had a new wheelchair, and her daughter-in-law could push her to church and other community activities. A new tukul had been built for her and she looked much happier and healthier.

Mama Susan constantly faces many expectations of those in the community and the challenges of a growing organization. She continues to rise to these challenges. She faced criticism over advocating for some children in prison to be released. She and local pastors have gone to the prisons to speak out for those they feel have been unjustly imprisoned or mistreated. At Christmas, she has been known to take large amounts of food to feed the prisoners.

Susan has over 150 orphans in her care between St. Bartholomew's, Amazing Grace, and her home in Kampala. Providing enough food, clothing, and funds for school fees has been a huge and unrelenting struggle. At times the children and staff have gone hungry or barely had enough food. Susan has learned to live "on the edge" for most of her faith journey.

Several young people have been inspired through the Lahash website to live in Sudan and Uganda, helping Mama Susan for longer periods of time. Some of them made several trips or stayed for extended periods, like Ashley and José, who stayed nearly a year.

One thing all these young people seem to have in common is that they love, admire, and respect Mama Susan. They have caught her God-given vision and are putting their time and resources to work to help her. Videos, photography, writing, and art are all combined to inform people of the needs of Susan and other partners, connect sponsors and children, and increase the flow of communication.

Lahash has a child sponsorship program and other projects to help with the care of the children. For example, they developed Rice & Beans Month as an act of solidarity with the children in Uganda and Sudan. Participants choose to eat rice and beans for one meal, one whole day, or for an entire month, and then send the surplus grocery money to Lahash to help fund food projects in East Africa. Rice & Beans Month was an immense help to Susan and Amazing Grace Children's Home, as over 200 people participated and nearly $6,000 was raised in 2010. The results were astounding as Dan and other visitors were able to see how much healthier and well nourished the children appeared compared to previous years.

The partnership between Mama Susan and Lahash has created an environment where it is possible to learn from one another and participate together to meet the needs of the children. It has been a struggle at times, but the mutual benefits in understanding and growth have been extraordinary. The tasks they have accomplished together have done much to not only save and improve the lives of the children, but help prepare them for the future as well.

In Susan's words, "These children were once like animals. They lived without love. Now they are doing well in school. They were miserable without school. Now there is hope that they will become responsible. They listen. They know God. They know His forgiveness. They know what love is. They are happy. And it is better to struggle with them than to be without them." Although partnering with Lahash and other groups has multiplied the accomplishments, much is still yet to be done.

There are still some worries that Sudan will erupt in violence, even if in sporadic areas. The South voted to secede from the North in an overwhelming referendum vote in January 2011. The new nation's first Independence Day celebration was July 9, 2011. Susan's resources will be stretched to the limit if there is increased violence and unrest. In that case, Susan may have to relocate the children out of Sudan, which would be a costly and difficult undertaking.

"I was hungry and you gave Me food; I was thirsty and you gave Me drink; I was a stranger and you took Me in; I was naked and you clothed Me; I was sick and you visited Me; I was in prison and you came to Me." – Matthew 25:35-36

12

NO MORE DYING THERE?
Hopes for a Peaceful Sudan

"Silence in the face of evil is itself evil.
Not to act is to act.
Not to speak is to speak."
– Dietrich Bonhoeffer

It was a bright, sunny day on February 8, 2008, just a few days after those fearful nights at the orphanage and worrying about LRA attacks. Our spirits were high as we had a truckload of bags of grain and other food and medical supplies to distribute. The UN had cleared our trip, even though we were passing near a village that had been attacked just a few days before.

The radio was on full blast, playing an English rendition of a gospel song. Some of the words touched me deeply: "No more crying there...no more dying there..."

Tears were misting in my eyes. We had been making our way, weaving and dipping, the lorry full of food for the people with leprosy in Magiri.

The touching thing to me was that we were following huge UN trucks transporting refugees back to Sudan from refugee camps in Uganda. The people were packed in tight with their few scant belongings – all their worldly goods. In some cases this included goats and other animals, along with their packages of household items.

I was crammed into the front of the lorry along with a nurse from Canada, a few staff, and the driver, Patrick. The young volunteers and some of the children and staff were all riding on the back of the open air truck with the food.

As the song played over and over, I thought about the refugees coming back after years of waiting, coming back to their precious homeland that was so impoverished and poorly developed. Would they be able to survive? Would war or violence break out again and take their lives or those of their family? Would there be more dying there? More crying there?

Mama Susan's faith has been stretched by war and immense needs many times, and it will be so again. She has chosen to stay and face the fear of war and to do what she can to prepare herself and the children. She needs her brothers and sisters in Christ from around the world to stand with her and provide for and protect the children, to advocate on their behalf.

"Open your mouth for the speechless, in the cause of all who are appointed to die. Open your mouth, judge righteously, and plead the cause of the poor and needy." – Proverbs 31:8-9

UN trucks transporting refugees back home to Sudan

APPENDIX

REBUILDING THE WALLS

"Let us rise up and build." – Nehemiah 2:18

South Sudan celebrated independence from Sudan on July 9, 2011. There is continued unrest and sporadic violence, especially as most of the oil reserves are in the South. The North has been accused of arming groups such as the LRA to provoke fear and instability.

During the fearful week I spent at St. Bartholomew's, I became acutely aware of the vulnerability of the orphanage. The Nile crossing, with its erratic ferry service, would be easy to commandeer and any route to escape could be blocked off. The city of Kajo Keji appears defenseless. The UN compound there was walled off with a few people inside. I have heard that in many parts of Sudan, they use "arrow boys" to defend the people because the local police and armed services are so lacking in people and equipment. It wouldn't take much to overpower and take over the orphanages and the town.

A recent letter from Mama Susan highlights the preparations she is making. The landlord at Amazing Grace wants his land back, so she has been working to find a new site for the orphanage. She is looking to get new land and at the same time build accommodations for all the children from St. Bartholomew's if they have to be evacuated from Sudan. The man who funded the home for babies visited Uganda in December 2010 to look with Susan for a possible place to relocate if needed.

Susan writes, "If we plan wisely, I believe the land... will accommodate 150 people. We could build double-storied buildings and still have space for planting. We share the area with a new primary school, and the children can share the playground with the primary school."

She also wants to rent or build a large room in Adjumani and stock it with maize, sorghum, beans and groundnuts for marketing. They have the opportunity to purchase land nearby for farming crops to be sold as well to provide food for the children.

Susan also alludes to security issues, even at Amazing Grace: "We all know that the LRA are still on the run, and might resume fighting and capturing people at any time. We had better stay in a small but secure development rather than living in fear on a larger piece of land." This comment was made in relation to the option of purchasing a larger piece of land away from the city, where the children would be more exposed.

Lahash and others who have met Susan are willing to help, but much additional help will be needed to protect and sustain the children.

If you would like to find out more about Mama Susan and how you can help rebuild the wall, contact Lahash International at www.lahash.org.

For more information about IWASSRU and how to

purchase fair trade items, do an internet search for the term "IWASSRU." You will also find many excellent photos of Susan's projects at "100 Cameras."

For more information on some of the topics in this story, view the movies "War Dance," "War Child," "Invisible Children," and "Lost Boys of Sudan."

Last updated July 2011

ACKNOWLEDGEMENTS

Thanks to the many that have helped put this story together. Thanks especially to Dan Holcomb and Todd Werkhoven of Lahash who helped edit and rewrite large portions. Thanks to Casey Schilperoort for cover design and interior layout, Nate Grubbs for photos, and Dana Bertermann for editing help. Thank you to Jen Johnson for amazing editing and copyediting help, and also to Eunice Reynolds for copyediting help.

Thanks to my mother, Ruby Pew, and daughter, Lisa Labon, who also spent many hours reading and rereading and giving excellent feedback.

Thanks also to Kudzai Marufu and Patience Mbiya for help with the African perspective.

Thank you to Claudia McGeary, founder of Faith in Africa, for your editing help and ideas for improving the story's flow.

A special thanks to my friends Jochannah Holman, Christy Wilner, Shirley O'Farrell, Kathy Miller, and Theresa Lee who read and critiqued it for me, and to the many of you who helped me choose a title.

A special thank you to José Nunez and Ashley Eggert for your labor of love in helping Susan for a year, and for sharing your faith with me during that fearful week at St. Bartholomew's.

Also thanks and appreciation to Ron and Char Holcomb, Dan's parents and long term missionaries with Africa Inland Mission. Thank you for serving in Juba,

Sudan, with your young family in those years of civil war. Thank you for traveling with me on that last trip and for being such an amazing inspiration of faith, love, and perseverance. Thank you, Ron, for sharing your storytelling knowledge and expertise. And Char, for always being there with love, encouragement, and Biblical wisdom for all.

Lyla stands next to Mama Susan for a photograph of the Lahash team during their visit to St. Bartholomew's in Sudan

9602288R1004

Made in the USA
Charleston, SC
26 September 2011